A Beginning-to-Read Book

Being Kind to Animals

by Mary Lindeen

NORWOOD HOUSE PRESS

DEAR CAREGIVER, The *Beginning to Read—Read and Discover* books provide emergent readers the opportunity to explore the world through nonfiction while building early reading skills. The text integrates both common sight words and content vocabulary. These key words are featured on lists provided at the back of the book to help your child expand his or her sight word recognition, which helps build reading fluency. The content words expand vocabulary and support comprehension.

Nonfiction text is any text that is factual. The Common Core State Standards call for an increase in the amount of informational text reading among students. The Standards aim to promote college and career readiness among students. Preparation for college and career endeavors requires proficiency in reading complex informational texts in a variety of content areas. You can help your child build a foundation by introducing nonfiction early. To further support the CCSS, you will find Reading Reinforcement activities at the back of the book that are aligned to these Standards.

Above all, the most important part of the reading experience is to have fun and enjoy it!

Sincerely,

Shannon Cannon

Shannon Cannon, Ph.D.
Literacy Consultant

Norwood House Press

For more information about Norwood House Press please visit our website at www.norwoodhousepress.com or call 866-565-2900.
© 2021 Norwood House Press. Beginning-to-Read™ is a trademark of Norwood House Press. All rights reserved. No part of this book may be reproduced or utilized in any form or by any means without written permission from the publisher.

Editor: Judy Kentor Schmauss
Designer: Sara Radka

Photo Credits:
Getty Images, cover, 3, 5, 6, 6, 7, 10, 13, 14, 17, 18, 22, 25, 26, 27, 29; Pixabay, 21; Shutterstock, 1, 9

Library of Congress Cataloging-in-Publication Data
Names: Lindeen, Mary, author.
Title: Being kind to animals / by Mary Lindeen.
Description: Chicago : Norwood House Press, [2021] | Series: A beginning to read book | Audience: Grades K-1 | Summary: "Describes what we can do to be kind to both tame and wild animals, such as being gentle and patient and learning how to give them what they need so they can grow and thrive. An early social-emotional learning book that includes a note to caregivers, reading activities, and a word list"— Provided by publisher.
Identifiers: LCCN 2019048860 (print) | LCCN 2019048861 (ebook) | ISBN 9781684508952 (hardcover) | ISBN 9781684045150 (paperback) | ISBN 9781684045198 (epub)
Subjects: LCSH: Humane education—Juvenile literature. | Animals—Juvenile literature. | Kindness—Juvenile literature.
Classification: LCC HV4712 .L56 2021 (print) | LCC HV4712 (ebook) | DDC 179/.3—dc23
LC record available at https://lccn.loc.gov/2019048860
LC ebook record available at https://lccn.loc.gov/2019048861

Hardcover ISBN: 978-1-68450-895-2
Paperback ISBN: 978-1-68404-515-0

328N—072020
Manufactured in the United States of America in North Mankato, Minnesota.

People need animals.

Animals need
people, too.

They need our care
and kindness.

How can you be
kind to animals?

You can be gentle.

You can talk to them
in a calm voice.

You can pet them
with a soft touch.

You can be patient.

You can give
animals time to
get to know you.

You can wait
to pet them
until they come
to you.

You can keep
animals healthy.

You can make sure
they have food
and water.

You can give them
safe places
to sleep.

You can take them
to the vet.

Animals need
room to play
and explore.

You can give them
space to move
around in.

You can be kind to
wild animals, too.

Being too close
or too loud
can scare them.

So watch them
quietly from
a distance.

Eating food made for people or pets can make wild animals sick.

So don't feed them.

Wild animals that
are sick or hurt
can be scared
or angry.

So stay away
from them.

Ask an adult
for help instead.

How can you be kind to all animals?

You can learn more about them.

Then you'll know what animals need to be healthy, safe, and happy.

You can take care of our planet.

Then animals can have a
safe, healthy world to live in.

What's the best thing about being kind to animals?

You might just make a new friend!

. . . READING REINFORCEMENT. . .

CRAFT AND STRUCTURE

To check your child's understanding of the organization of the book, recreate the following chart on a sheet of paper. Read the book with your child, and then help him or her fill in the chart using what they learned. Work together to complete the chart by writing words or ideas from the book that tell about ways to be kind to animals.

Being Kind to Animals

VOCABULARY: Learning Content Words

Content words are words that are specific to a particular topic. All of the content words in this book can be found on page 32. Use some or all of these content words to complete one or more of the following activities:

• Play "Jeopardy" with your child. Ask questions for which the content words are the answers; for example, "What is a word that means 'not sick'?"

• Ask your child questions about the words that begin with "Who?" "What?" "Where?" "When?" "Why?" and "How?"

• Say a word and have your child say the first word that comes to his or her mind. Talk about his or her answer.

• Ask your child to draw pictures of words he or she has difficulty remembering the meaning to.

• Have your child find smaller words or word parts within the words.

FOUNDATIONAL SKILLS: Suffixes

A *suffix* is a letter or group of letters added to the end of a word to change its meaning or to form a different word. Have your child identify the suffixes in the list below. Then help your child find words with suffixes in this book.

frightful	happiness	lazy
enjoyment	friendly	likeable

CLOSE READING OF INFORMATIONAL TEXT

Close reading helps children comprehend text. It includes reading a text, discussing it with others, and answering questions about it. Use these questions to discuss this book with your child:

- Why should you use a soft touch when petting animals?
- What do animals need to stay healthy?
- What should you not do with wild animals?
- What might happen if you feed "people food" to animals?
- What does "being patient" mean?
- How are *you* kind to your pets or other people's pets?

FLUENCY

Fluency is the ability to read accurately with speed and expression. Help your child practice fluency by using one or more of the following activities:

- Reread the book to your child at least two times while he or she uses a finger to track each word as it is read.
- Read a line of the book, then reread it as your child reads along with you.
- Ask your child to go back through the book and read the words he or she knows.
- Have your child practice reading the book several times to improve accuracy, rate, and expression.

··· Word List ···

Being Kind to Animals uses the 98 words listed below. *High-frequency words* are those words that are used most often in the English language. They are sometimes referred to as *sight words* because children need to learn to recognize them automatically when they read. *Content words* are any words specific to a particular topic. Regular practice reading these words will enhance your child's ability to read with greater fluency and comprehension.

High-Frequency Words

a	can	in	people	thing
about	come	know	place(s)	time
all	eat(ing)	live	play	to
an	for	made	so	too
and	from	make	take	until
are	get	more	that	water
around	give	new	the	what
ask	have	of	them	with
away	help	or	then	world
be(ing)	how	our	they	you

Content Words

adult	feed	kind(ness)	room	touch
angry	friend	learn	safe	vet
animals	food	loud	scare(d)	voice
best	gentle	might	sick	wait
calm	happy	move	sleep	watch
care	healthy	need	soft	what's
close	hurt	patient	space	wild
distance	instead	pet(s)	stay	you'll
don't	just	planet	sure	
explore	keep	quietly	talk	

••• About the Author

Mary Lindeen is a writer, editor, parent, and former elementary school teacher. She has written more than 100 books for children and edited many more. She specializes in early literacy instruction and books for young readers, especially nonfiction.